POSTCARD HISTORY SERIES

Gettysburg

VINTAGE POSTCARD VIEWS OF AMERICA'S GREATEST BATTLEFIELD

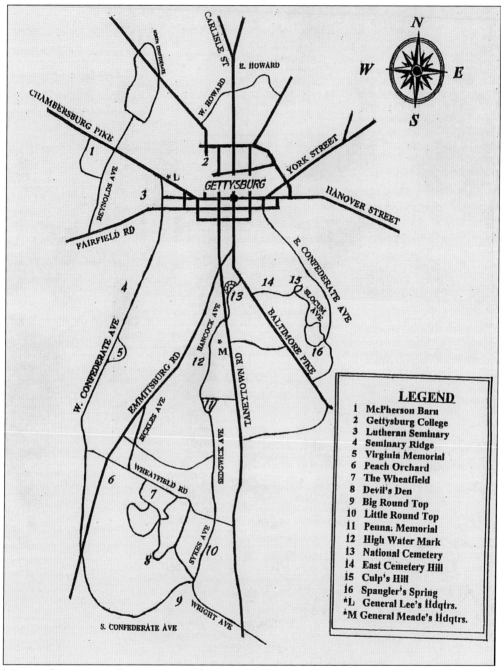

MAP OF GETTYSBURG BATTLEFIELD. This simplified map will serve to orient the reader to key sites and landmarks on the battlefield.

LEGEND

1 McPherson Barn
2 Gettysburg College
3 Lutheran Seminary
4 Seminary Ridge
5 Virginia Memorial
6 Peach Orchard
7 The Wheatfield
8 Devil's Den
9 Big Round Top
10 Little Round Top
11 Penna. Memorial
12 High Water Mark
13 National Cemetery
14 East Cemetery Hill
15 Culp's Hill
16 Spangler's Spring
*L General Lee's Hdqtrs.
*M General Meade's Hdqtrs.

POSTCARD HISTORY SERIES

Gettysburg

VINTAGE POSTCARD VIEWS OF AMERICA'S GREATEST BATTLEFIELD

James D. Ristine

ARCADIA
PUBLISHING

Published by Arcadia Publishing
Charleston, South Carolina

Printed in the United States of America

Library of Congress Catalog Card Number: Applied for.

For all general information contact Arcadia Publishing at:
Telephone 843-853-2070
Fax 843-853-0044
E-mail sales@arcadiapublishing.com
For customer service and orders:
Toll-Free 1-888-313-2665

Visit us on the Internet at www.arcadiapublishing.com

I would like to dedicate this book to my great-grandfather, John C. Casner of Duncansville, Pennsylvania. He served his country from February 1862 until July of 1865 as a sergeant in Company H of the 12th Regiment Pennsylvania Volunteer Cavalry.

CONTENTS

IN MEMORY. The Civil War lasted from 1861 to 1865 and pitted American against American. This Decoration Day postcard from the early 1900s honors the soldiers of both the North and South who fought valiantly for their respective causes. (T.P. & Co., c. 1905.)

ACKNOWLEDGMENTS

In undertaking the writing of this book I attempted to blend my interest in history with my passion for collecting, especially the collecting of postcards (deltiology). Assisting me in my efforts were a number of people who graciously gave of their time and expertise. These individuals include Donald Brown of the Institute of American Deltiology located in Myerstown, Pennsylvania. He shared with me his enthusiasm for postcards and was kind enough to allow me to use several postcards for inclusion in this book. Another person who provided me information in regards to the publishers of Gettysburg postcards was Dr. Richard Sauers. Tim Smith and Dr. Michael McGough, both of whom are authors and Licensed Battlefield Guides, gave me the benefit of their vast knowledge on the subject of the battlefield. Thanks also to Jim Luty, who provided me with a postcard from his personal collection that pictures noted battlefield guide Capt. James T. Long. The Adams County Historical Society located in Gettysburg also proved very helpful in my research.

Most of all I wish to thank my loving wife, Debbie, who helped in the proofreading of the text and whose encouragement made this personal endeavor possible.

Lastly, acknowledgment is due to the many photographers and publishers of the postcard views that are found in this book. It is their work which has helped record and preserve through visual images this incredible American treasure known as the Gettysburg Battlefield.

INTRODUCTION

During the early spring of 1863 the small town of Gettysburg, with a population of 2,400 people, was best known as the county seat of Adams County, Pennsylvania, home to a Lutheran Theological Seminary and a small college. Most people outside of south central Pennsylvania were probably unfamiliar with this rural community only 8 miles from the famed Mason Dixon line. This relative anonymity, however, was to change forever in early July of that fateful year.

The American Civil War had been going on for two years when Gen. Robert E. Lee, commander of the Confederate Army of Northern Virginia, decided to take the war to the Northern states. With the capture of Harrisburg, Pennsylvania, as an objective, Lee hoped to achieve a number of vital military and political goals. As his formidable army marched north through the Pennsylvania countryside in June of 1863, his enemy, the Union Army of the Potomac (which would soon be under command of Gen. George G. Meade) was approaching from the south and east. Although not the initial choice of either commander for the site of battle, fate would have it that these two massive armies would converge on the small town of Gettysburg on the first day of July. The military encounter that resulted involved fighting that took place over approximately 25 square miles of terrain in and around the town. Before it was over, more than 172,000 soldiers of the Confederate and Union armies would engage in combat. During July 1, 2, and 3, in what has become known as the Battle of Gettysburg, an estimated 51,000 men would be killed, wounded, captured, or recorded as missing. Thus Gettysburg became the location of the largest and bloodiest battle ever fought on American soil. The events that occurred here would culminate in the "high tide" of the Confederacy and mark the turning point of the Civil War.

It is said that the Battle of Gettysburg is one of the most written-about and analyzed conflicts in world history. The purpose of this book is to present its dramatic story in a unique and hopefully interesting manner. This book will explore the events of the battle, the battlefield, and the town itself, through the use of vintage postcards that were published from 1900 through the early 1920s. By way of the images depicted on these postcards, you the reader will embark on an exploration of this, one of America's most significant battles and landmarks. The images will enable you to visit the town where the hostilities took place, follow the sequence of the major events of the battle, and look upon the battlefield sites where our nation's fate was decided. You will also visit the National Cemetery which serves as the final resting place for many of those who fell in battle, see the monuments erected to honor those of both sides who fought here, and take note of the veterans, tourists, and others who have come to this "hallowed ground" and become part of the history of what we know as the Gettysburg National Military Park.

For the benefit of postcard collectors I have included (when known) the name of the publisher, card number, and the date or estimated date of publication. Postcards have long been utilized as souvenirs or as an easy way to send a thought or remembrance to a friend or loved one as well as serve as a snapshot of history. Through postcards we can document how things once looked and thereby see the changes that have occurred over the years.

The reader of this book who visits the battlefield will surely notice that many of the views depicted on these postcards have changed. Some roadways have been modified, added, or even removed. Other monuments have been erected, and trees and vegetation have altered the panorama of the battleground. But one thing has remained the same over the decades—the battlefield that we see portrayed on the many postcards in this book (and the battlefield seen by the modern visitor) stands as a tribute and lasting remembrance to all those, from the North and South, who fought here in the summer of 1863.

SOUVENIR FROM THE BATTLEFIELD. To visitors in the early 1900s, postcards such as this made an inexpensive souvenir or remembrance to send to friends or relatives. Over the years, tens of millions of people have made the journey to Gettysburg to view the battlefield where our nation's destiny was determined. (Pub. unknown; *c.* 1900.)

One

THE TOWN OF GETTYSBURG

BATTLEFIELD OF GETTYSBURG.
AS IT WAS IN 1863.

1. Emmitsburg Road.	3. Hagerstown Road (Fairfield)	5. Mummasburg Road.	7. Harrisburg Road.	9. York Pike.	11. Baltimore Pike
2. Millerstown Road.	4. Chambersburg Pike (Cashtown)	6. Carlisle Road.	8. Hunterstown Road.	10. Hanover Road.	12. Taneytown Ro

Round Top.   Devil's Den.   Wheat Field.   Peach Orchard.   Pickett's Woods.   McPherson's Woods.
Little   The Angle.   Seminary   Oak Hill.
Round Top.   Meade's   Cemetery   Gettysburg
Headquarters.   Hill.
Power's Hill.   Culp's Hill.   Barlow Knoll.

Photographed from Huidekoper's Relief Map. Copyright, 1901, by H. S. HUIDEKOPER. Area, 5 x 3½ miles.

BATTLEFIELD RELIEF MAP. H.S. Huidekoper's relief map of Gettysburg clearly shows how the ten major roads leading into town looked much like the spokes of a wheel. Because of these converging routes, and the fact that the town lay in the paths of the Army of the Potomac and the Army of Northern Virginia, the town of Gettysburg was destined to become the site of our nation's greatest Civil War battle. (W.H. Tipton, #219; c. 1901.)

GETTYSBURG FROM NORTH CONFEDERATE AVENUE. Founded in 1780 by James Gettys, for whom the town was named, Gettysburg consisted of approximately 450 buildings and had a population of 2,400 in 1863. As the county seat of Adams County, the town also boasted a Lutheran Seminary and a small college. Here the town can be seen to the south of what is now North Confederate Avenue. (W.H. Tipton, multiview set; c. 1905.)

GETTYSBURG BATTLEFIELD. In this view we look to the south upon land that was to become the site of the greatest military engagement ever to take place in North America. In the distance can be seen the heights known as the Round Tops, while in the foreground lies the flat farmland that became part of the battlefield. Gettysburg offered both armies a variety of terrain on which to do battle. (Raphael Tuck & Sons, ser. #1080; c. 1905.)

GETTYSBURG FROM OBSERVATION TOWER ON OAK HILL. Here we see the town of Gettysburg from yet another perspective. In the center we see the town, while Culp's Hill, which was to become the right flank of the Union line, is seen to the left. On the far right are the Round Tops, which anchored the southern end of the Union line on the second and third day of battle. (W.H. Tipton, #221; 1909.)

CENTER SQUARE. Like many small Pennsylvania towns, Gettysburg possesses a center square into which four major streets converge. On July 1, 1863, Union troops of the 1st and 11th Corps fled through this town center on their way to Cemetery Hill, to the south. Fighting was to occur here and along the streets and alleys as Union soldiers were driven down Baltimore Street. (David Kaufman, #102527: c. 1915.)

HOTEL GETTYSBURG, GETTYSBURG, PA.

HOTEL GETTYSBURG. Hotel Gettysburg, seen here in the early 1900s, is located on the Center Square. This building has been used for hotel purposes since 1797 and has hosted a long list of distinguished patrons. After a devastating fire in 1983, the structure was rebuilt. It still functions as a hotel. (Louis Kaufmann & Sons, #R-38500; *c.* 1915.)

YORK STREET. Running eastward from the town square, York Street, also known today as Route 30, heads towards the city of York, Pennsylvania, 28 miles away. It was along this street that some of the Confederate troops entered the town on July 1, 1863. (Rotograph Co., #E-3719a; c. 1907.)

CARLISLE STREET. Running north from the center square, Carlisle Street is one of the four major thoroughfares in town. On the first day of battle it served as one of the routes by which Confederate troops entered Gettysburg and along which Union soldiers fled. It is on this street, just down from the square, that the railroad station is located. (W.H. Tipton, #209; c. 1908.)

RAILROAD STATION. This railroad station, located on the northwest corner of Washington and Railroad Streets, was built by the Gettysburg and Harrisburg Railroad in 1884 to help increase accessibility for tourists coming to visit the battlefield. A short distance away, the Carlisle Street railroad depot, built in 1858 in the Italinate Villa style of architecture, has seen much history. It served as a hospital early in the battle. After the conflict, two trains per day carried the many wounded home or on to treatment centers. It was here, on Nevomber 18, 1863, that President Lincoln arrived from Washington, D. C., to participate in the dedication of The National Cemetery. (Union News Co., #1151; c. 1910.)

EAGLE HOTEL. Located along Chambersburg Street, this historic building was built in the early 1830s. After the Civil War it was considered by many to be the town's leading hotel. In 1901 it had 300 guest rooms and its owner, Frank Eberhart, boasted of its being the only such establishment in town with private baths and elevator service for its patrons. (Rotograph Co., #E3716a; c. 1907.)

MAIN STREET. In this view of busy Chambersburg Street we get another perspective of the Eagle Hotel. Even in 1863, this street was home to a number of businesses. On the first day of battle, the Southern forces approaching from the west entered the town by way of this street. (Union News Co., #1137; c. 1910.)

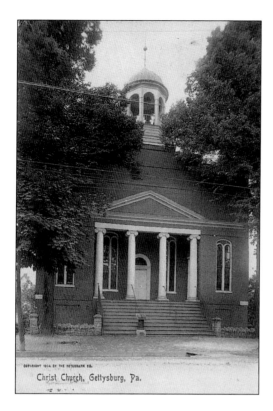

Christ Church, Gettysburg, Pa.

CHRIST CHURCH. Situated along Chambersburg Street, near the center of town, this Lutheran church dates to 1836. In front of the building can be seen a tablet in memory of Chaplain Horatio S. Howell of the 90th Pa. Infantry. While walking down the steps of the church on July 1, 1863, he was shot by an approaching Confederate soldier. At the time, the church was being used as a hospital. (Rotograph Co., #3707; 1904.)

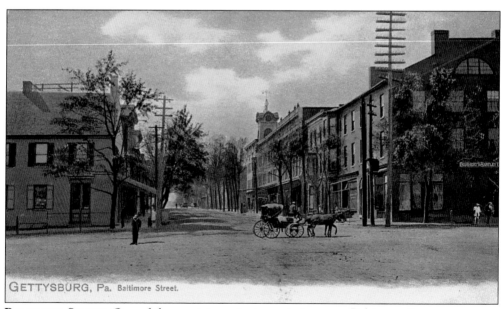

GETTYSBURG, Pa. Baltimore Street.

BALTIMORE STREET. One of the most important streets in town, Baltimore Street was to see much activity during the three days of battle. It was here, at noon on July 1, 1863, that Union forces advanced north towards the escalating conflict. And it was along this same route that they were to flee towards Cemetery Hill, when routed by the Confederate army later in the afternoon. (Raphael Tuck & Sons, ser. #2397; c. 1907.)

Memorial Church.   Gettysburg, Pa.

PRINCE OF PEACE CHURCH. Situated on the corner of Baltimore and High Streets, the Prince of Peace Episcopal Church was erected in 1900 on the site of the former David McCreary House. Like many churches, it has played a big part in the life of people in and around Gettysburg. As a result, most churches like this one contain plaques or memorials dedicated to participants of the battle. (American News Co., #A6604; c. 1907.)

THE HOME OF GEORGE P. BLACK, GETTYSBURG, PA., COMMONLY KNOWN AS THE « SWEENEY HOUSE »

SWEENEY HOUSE. Located along Baltimore Street, this house, known formerly as the "Sweeney House," was occupied by Confederate sharpshooters during the battle. Numerous bullet and shell holes still remain in the building. For years the home was owned by the Black family, who rented rooms to tourists. It is now restored and known as the Farnsworth House Inn. (Louis Kaufmann & Sons; c. 1910.)

17

GETTYSBURG COLLEGE. Established in 1832, Gettysburg College is the oldest Lutheran College in America. Originally part of the Lutheran Theological Seminary, it was known as Pennsylvania College in 1863. During and after the battle most of its buildings served as hospitals for the many wounded. (Louis Kaufmann & Sons, #36; *c.* 1907.)

GETTYSBURG, P
Recitation Hall
Gettysburg College

RECITATION HALL, GETTYSBURG COLLEGE. Recitation Hall, also known as Gladfelter Hall, was one of three principal buildings comprising Pennsylvania College in 1863. On the morning of July 1, classes were dismissed when the sounds of battle reached the school. At the time of the battle (and for a while afterward) this structure was utilized as a hospital. (Raphael Tuck & Sons, ser. #2397; *c.* 1907.)

Old Dorm, Gettysburg College. "Old Dorm," erected in 1838, had its cupola employed as an observation post and its rooms as a hospital during the battle. This building has the distinction of being one of just a small number of structures in our nation permitted by law to fly the American flag at night without illumination. (C.T. Photochrom, #R-37836; *c.* 1915.)

Meade High School. Built in 1897, the Meade High School stands at the juncture of Springs Avenue and Buford Avenue (Route 30). Just down the road, on the right, stands the Thompson house, which was to become General Lee's headquarters. The Lutheran Theological Seminary is also just a short distance away. (W.H. Tipton, #217; *c.* 1908.)

LUTHERAN THEOLOGICAL SEMINARY. Milton Valentine Hall is one of several buildings comprising the Lutheran Theological Seminary, which is located on the west end of town. This institution, one of the town's most noted features in 1863, gave the name Seminary Ridge to this locale. During the battle and for months after, these buildings were to serve as hospitals for the many wounded of both armies. (W.H. Tipton, multiview set; c. 1905.)

THEOLOGICAL SEMINARY. Schmucker Hall of the Lutheran Theological Seminary, seen here, was built in 1832. On the morning of the first day of battle its cupola was utilized by Generals Buford and Reynolds as an observation post. The building eventually fell to the Confederates, who continued to use it as an observatory and hospital. Since 1961 the building has served as the home of the Adams County Historical Society. (Louis Kaufmann & Sons, #15; c. 1907.)

DOBBIN HOUSE. Situated along Steinwehr Avenue, this building was built in 1776 by Rev. Alexander Dobbin for his wife and ten children. He later opened a Classical Academy (a combination seminary and liberal arts college) at the location. In the mid-1800s it functioned as a station on the Underground Railroad for runaway slaves. Today it is restored and serves to welcome visitors as the Dobbin House Tavern. (Rotograph Co., #E-3707a; c. 1907.)

ENTRANCE TO CITY CEMETERY. The gatehouse of Evergreen Cemetery, the civilian cemetery, was completed in 1855, just one year after the cemetery was opened. Much of the original brickwork of this entranceway still stands. It is this burial ground which gives Cemetery Hill its name. During the battle, heavy combat was to take place near this structure. (Rotograph Co., #3724; 1904.)

Wolf Hill. Located east of town and on the other side of Culp's Hill is a high, thickly wooded area of rough terrain known as Wolf Hill. This section of the battlefield was occupied by Neill's Brigade of the Union's 6th Corps. Their role was to protect the armies right flank and to serve as a reserve force. (W.H. Tipton, #S-653; 1906.)

McAllister's Dam, Rock Creek. Named for the large boulders along its banks and within its channel, Rock Creek is located just east of town. Running north to south and extending the length of the battlefield, this picturesque creek was forded numerous times by both Union and Confederate troops during the conflict. (W.H. Tipton, #212; c. 1908.)

Two

THE BATTLE DAY ONE
JULY 1, 1863

Statues of Gen. Buford, Gen. Reynolds and Hall's
2nd Maine Battery, Gettysburg, Pa.

MCPHERSON'S RIDGE. At approximately 8 a.m. on July 1, 1863, two brigades of dismounted Union cavalry commanded by Gen. John Buford engaged two advancing brigades of Confederate infantry of Gen. Henry Heth's Division. This initial encounter on McPherson's Ridge was soon to escalate into the largest battle of the Civil War. The cannon mounted at the base of Buford's statue are the very ones which fired the first Union artillery rounds of the conflict. (C.T. Photochrom, #R-37856; c. 1913.)

FIRST DAY'S FIGHT, REYNOLDS' WOODS. Early in the battle, around 10 a.m., Union Gen. John F. Reynolds was shot and killed while directing his troops at the edge of McPherson's Woods (since renamed Reynolds' Woods). Shortly after, General Meredith, leading the "Iron Brigade," attacked through the woods, successfully putting to flight Confederate troops under command of Gen. James Archer. Nearly 1,000 prisoners were taken, including General Archer. (J.I. Mumper; 1909.)

North Confederate Avenue, Gettysburg, Pa.

NORTH CONFEDERATE AVENUE. Immediately to the right of this view is where, early in the afternoon, a countercharge by Gen. Henry Baxter's Brigade virtually destroyed Confederate General Iverson's Brigade. Within a 15-minute period, a brigade of 1,384 men was reduced to no more than 400; the rest were either killed or captured. (C.T. Photochrom, #R-37832; c. 1913.)

THE McPHERSON BARN. The 150th Pennsylvania Volunteer Infantry known as the "Bucktail" Brigade is shown behind a split-rail fence, attempting to repel a Confederate attack. After suffering extremely high casualties, they were driven from the battlefield. The barn was later to be used as a hospital. (Rotograph Co., #E-3720a; *c.* 1907.)

STORMING OF THE BARN. The McPherson barn, situated along the Chambersburg Pike, was the scene of intense fighting. This postcard depicts the afternoon attack by Confederate troops of Col. John Brockenbrough's Virginian Brigade. The Confederates were successful in driving away the Pennsylvania Bucktails, who were defending the barn and its surrounding ground. (A.C. Bosselman & Co., #13008; *c.* 1910.)

JOHN BURNS STATUE. Upon hearing the sounds of battle, John Burns, a citizen reputed to have been over 70 years of age, took up his gun to help repel the rebel attackers. Here, along the edge of Reynolds' Woods, near the McPherson barn, he joined the skirmishing line of the 150th Pennsylvania Regiment, and later that day, the 2nd Wisconsin. He was to be wounded three times before the day was finished. (C.T. Photochrom, #R-37839; c. 1913.)

JOHN L. BURNS HOME. John Burns became known as the "Hero of Gettysburg" for his actions on the first day of the battle. In this picture, from a photograph taken in July of 1863, we see Burns on the porch of his home, recovering from his battle wounds. In later years he was to serve as the town's constable. Death finally claimed him in 1872, and he is now buried in Evergreen Cemetery. (W.H. Tipton, #5875; c. 1915.)

HOWARD AVENUE. The Union 11th Corps arrived at this location north of town around noon on this first day of battle. After hurriedly being put into position, they were exposed to heavy artillery fire and then attacked by a superior force of Confederate infantry. (J.I. Mumper; 1909.)

HOWARD AVENUE AND BARLOW'S KNOLL. This view along Howard Avenue shows the relatively flat ground where the Union 11th Corps defended their battle line until about 3:30 p.m. Around that time the Union line broke and the Confederate army drove them through town and back to positions on Cemetery Hill. (W.H. Tipton, #302; c. 1910.)

13024 GENERAL ROBERT E. LEE

GEN. ROBERT E. LEE. Son of Revolutionary War hero "Lighthorse" Harry Lee, Robert E. Lee was appointed commander of the Army of Northern Virginia on June 1, 1862. He was to remain an idolized and beloved leader of his army, even after his defeat at Gettysburg. Lee is shown here mounted on "Traveller," his famous iron-gray horse, who carried him throughout the war. (Detroit Pub. Co., #13024; *c.* 1910.)

General Robert E. Lee and Staff, Gettysburg, Pa.

GEN. ROBERT E. LEE AND STAFF. Gen. Robert E. Lee, commander of the Army of Northern Virginia, arrived on the battlefield late in the afternoon. By this time the Union 1st and 11th Corps had been routed and was re-organizing on Cemetery Hill. Confederate lines were to stretch in a semicircle about 6 miles long to the north and west, while the Union army was consolidating its defensive line in the shape of a fish hook that measured about 3 miles in length. (C.T. Photochrom, #R-37844; *c.* 1913.)

General Lee's Headquarters, Chambersburg Pike, Gettysburg Battlefield, Pa.

GENERAL LEE'S HEADQUARTERS. This picturesque, small stone farmhouse constructed in 1779 was the home of the widow Mrs. Mary Thompson. It is situated near the crest of Seminary Ridge and fronts directly on the Chambersburg Pike (now Route 30), within sight of the Lutheran Seminary. (Union News Co., #M-3111; c. 1910.)

GENERAL LEE'S HEADQUARTERS. Here is another view of the building which served for a short time during the battle as General Lee's command post. The general himself actually slept in a tent pitched nearby. Today the building houses the General Lee's Headquarters Museum. (Interstate News Co., #G-37; c. 1916.)

GENERAL MEADE'S HEADQUARTERS. Very late on the night of July 1, Gen. George Meade arrived from Taneytown, Maryland. He established his headquarters in this tiny farmhouse, which was only 16 by 20 feet square. It was from here, the home of the widow Mrs. Leister, that Meade directed his army on the second and third days of battle. (C.T. Photochrom, #R-37842; c. 1913.)

GENERAL MEADE'S HEADQUARTERS. Here we see a rear view of the Leister House, which served as General Meade's headquarters. On the third day of battle, the general and his staff were forced to evacuate the house because of the intense cannonade prior to Pickett's Charge. The bombardment was so severe that 27 horses of his headquarters' guard were killed at this site. (Hugh C. Leighton, #4747; c. 1908.)

Three

THE BATTLE DAY TWO
JULY 2, 1863

Copyright 1904 by the Rotograph Co.

G 3712 General view from little Round Top, looking across the Valley of Death to the wheat field, Statue of Gen. Warren in foreground, Gettysburg, Pa.

Had a long drive this morning. Carroll.

VIEW FROM LITTLE ROUND TOP. On the second day of combat General Meade was to utilize 210 of his regiments in order to firm up and defend his positions. General Lee was to use 86 of his regiments in attacking both flanks of the Union Line. Some of the heaviest fighting of the day took place over the landscape seen in this view. (Rotograph Co., #G-3712; 1904.)

GEN. GEORGE MEADE AND CORPS COMMANDERS. In this reproduction of an authentic U.S. War Department photograph we see Gen. George Meade and his staff. General Meade assumed command of the Army of the Potomac on June 28, 1863. Little did he realize that the decisions he would make and actions he would take in just a few days time would ultimately determine the outcome of the Civil War. (A.C. Bosselman & Co., #13000; c. 1910.)

GEN. GEORGE G. MEADE AND STAFF. This painting by F.A. Wendroth portrays Gen. George G. Meade consulting with his staff officers while in the midst of battle. Meade would ultimately command a military force of approximately 95,000 men here at Gettysburg, in what was to be essentially a defensive battle for the Northern troops. (A.C. Bosselman & Co., #11465; c. 1910.)

LITTLE AND BIG ROUND TOPS. These two hills, known respectively as Little Round Top and Big Round Top, are the dominating heights on the southern end of the battlefield. Little Round Top would prove to be the more strategic of the two and would be heavily fought over on the second day. (Hugh C. Leighton, #4738; *c.* 1908.)

BIG ROUND TOP. With an elevation of 786 feet, Big Round Top is higher than Little Round Top, but because it was heavily wooded and steeply sloped, it was not very suitable for either infantry or artillery. However, troops did occupy the heights at times, and Law's Alabama Brigade advanced along the northern slope of this promontory on its way to assault Little Round Top. (W.H. Tipton, #310; *c.* 1910.)

33

Gettysburg, Pa, Little Round Top.

LITTLE ROUND TOP. Viewed from Devil's Den, Little Round Top is seen as a relatively steep, rocky slope. Just a year before the battle, its timber had been cleared by the landowner. This made it possible for anyone on top of the summit to command a large area of the southern end of the battlefield. It was because of this feature that possession of the peak was so vital and thus the reason why it was so heavily fought over. (Hugh C. Leighton, #4735; c. 1908.)

SIGNAL ROCK ON LITTLE ROUND TOP. Signal Rock was the location of the Union Army's first occupation of Little Round Top. From here the signal corpsmen observed enemy movements down below and communicated this information to other Federal positions. It was while visiting this station that Gen. G.K. Warren saw the need to immediately fortify these heights before their capture by Confederate forces. (American News Co., #A-6608; c. 1907.)

LITTLE ROUND TOP. After seeing the necessity of occupying Little Round Top, General Warren hastily ordered two elements of the 5th Corps, Vincent's Brigade, and Lieutenant Hazlett's artillery battery to secure the high ground. These troops reached the summit only minutes before a Confederate assault by General Law's Alabamians. For his quick action General Warren is remembered as "the savior of Little Round Top." (David Kaufman, #110968; c. 1920.)

LITTLE ROUND TOP. The crest of Little Round Top is seen here from the perspective of Sykes Avenue. Had the Confederate army been successful in occupying these heights, the outcome of the battle surely would have been much different. From this vantage point their artillery could have devastated the Union lines to the north. (David Kaufman, #102524; *c.* 1920.)

BETWEEN THE ROUNDTOPS. Confederate infantry crossed here between the roundtops on their way to storm the heights of Little Round Top. The 83rd Pennsylvania Regiment rushed in to try to halt the attack. Its commander, Col. Strong Vincent, was killed at a spot only a short distance behind where this monument now stands. Only the timely arrival of the 140th New York Regiment helped to break up the assault. (W.H. Tipton, #210; *c.* 1908.)

36

ETTYSBURG, Pa. Gen. Warren's Statue. Little Round Top.

LITTLE ROUND TOP. From Little Round Top the Union soldiers overlooked Devil's Den, the Wheatfield, and the Peach Orchard, all areas of heavy conflict on July 2. This formidable position anchored the left of the Union's defensive lines. The Confederates attempted several assaults on these heights and it was only by a determined and courageous effort that the defenders were able to hold this vital high ground. (Raphael Tuck & Sons, ser. #2397; c. 1907.)

BIG ROUND TOP, FROM DEVIL'S DEN. Big Round Top is viewed here from the rear of Devil's Den. As the Confederates were advancing towards Little Round Top, Union infantry and Capt. James Smith's 4th New York Battery (stationed here on Houck's Ridge) attempted to turn them back. (A.C. Bosselman & Co., #11725; c. 1910.)

SMITH'S 4TH NEW YORK BATTERY. As intense fighting developed in the Devil's Den area, Smith's Battery of four cannon was overrun by Gen. Henry L. Benning's Georgians. After capturing three of the fieldpieces the Confederates went on to drive the Union soldiers out from the boulders of Devil's Den. Casualties were high on both sides during this crucial encounter. (Rotograph Co., #3703b; c. 1910.)

DEVIL'S DEN. On the west side of the Valley of Death, and just below Little Round Top, this natural fortification of large rocks and crevices was briefly held by Union soldiers. After capture by General Hood's Confederates, the area was utilized as a sniper's nest, as it afforded natural protection and a clear view of the summit of Little Round Top. (Raphael Tuck & Sons, ser. #1025; c. 1905.)

DEVIL'S DEN. Confederate sharpshooters hidden among the boulders of Devil's Den were responsible for inflicting numerous casualties on the Union officers and soldiers atop nearby Little Round Top. Among those killed before nightfall on July 2 were brigade commander Gen. Stephen Weed and artilleryman Lt. Charles Hazlett. The Confederates kept possession of the rocky roost until their retreat at the end of the battle. (Leighton & Valentine , #216926; c. 1913.)

VALLEY OF DEATH. After being driven from Devil's Den and the surrounding area, Union troops fought courageously on the marshy flatland at the base of Little Round Top, which was to be named the Valley of Death. The small creek, Plum Run, which flows through the center of this view, ran red with the blood of countless dead and wounded and thus became known as "Bloody Run." (A.C. Bosselman & Co., #11729; c. 1910.)

GETTYSBURG BATTLEFIELD. This view looks out over the Valley of Death to the Wheatfield and the Peach Orchard in the distance. Some of the fiercest fighting of the second day occurred in these areas of once peaceful farmland when Gen. Daniel Sickles extended his men out in advance of the rest of the Union defensive lines. (Detroit Pub. Co.; c. 1910.)

VALLEY OF DEATH AND THE WHEATFIELD. This postcard gives us yet another perspective of the Valley of Death and the Wheatfield from atop Little Round Top. From this vantage point Union soldiers could observe the brutal combat taking place below them on these fields of battle. (Louis Kaufmann & Sons, #38; c. 1907.)

PEACH ORCHARD. Assigned the task of defending the left of the Union lines, Gen. Daniel Sickles, in command of the 3rd Corps, took it upon himself to shift his 6,000 soldiers into an area that became known as the "Peach Orchard." A heavy assault by Woffard's and Barksdale's Confederate Brigades successfully captured the Peach Orchard. In this engagement General Sickles would lose his leg to an artillery shell. (W.H. Tipton, multiview set; c. 1905.)

THE WHEATFIELD. Upon this field, named for the ripened grain that was to be trampled and bloodied by battle, was fought some of the most chaotic and confusing close combat of the entire battle. The fighting here began when General Longstreet launched an all-out attack on the left flank of the Union line. (W.H. Tipton, #308; *c.* 1910.)

THE WHEATFIELD. On this flatland bordering the Peach Orchard, Confederate and Union soldiers fought a furious engagement often involving hand-to-hand combat. The soldiers circled and fought each other in what has been called the "Whirlpool of Battle." In the maelstrom of combat the field was to change hands at least six times before the Confederates finally were able to hold the site by the weight of numbers alone. (Leighton & Valentine, #216940; *c.* 1913.)

CULP'S HILL, FROM EAST CEMETERY HILL. Culp's Hill, to the east of Cemetery Hill, is seen here in the distance. This hill was one of several locations to which Union forces retreated during the rout of the first day. Here they constructed defensive works in preparation for an attack and secured the right flank of the Union lines. (Hugh C. Leighton, #4737; c. 1908.)

CULP'S HILL AND STEVENS KNOLL. On the evening of July 2, Confederate soldiers of Johnson's Brigade attacked Culp's Hill, successfully capturing the breastworks at the base of the hill. They were to hold these positions until the next morning. From nearby Stevens Knoll, Union artillery poured a devastating enfilading fire on the enemy as they attempted an assault on East Cemetery Hill. (W.H. Tipton, #306; c. 1910.)

EAST CEMETERY HILL. At the base of this hill two brigades of Union soldiers, part of Gen. Francis Barlow's 11th Corps, occupied the stone wall seen here. Both of these units experienced heavy combat during the first day and suffered heavy casualties. (Louis Kaufmann & Sons, #39; c. 1907.)

CHARGE OF THE LOUISIANA TIGERS. As evening began to fall, units of the Confederate "Louisiana Tigers" charged the fortifications at the base of East Cemetery Hill, breaking through the Union line. After driving their foe up the slope, they captured the hill just as darkness fell. Their victory, however, was brief, as the timely arrival of reinforcements from Hancock's 2nd Corps arrived to repulse the attack. (A.C. Bosselman & Co., #13007; c. 1910.)

STORMING OF CEMETERY HILL. The "Louisiana Tigers," known for their courage in battle, were driven back down the slope in fierce hand-to-hand combat. Union artillery fire from nearby Stevens Knoll also took a toll on their numbers. By the time the fighting ended, the "Tigers" were practically annihilated as a fighting force. (W.H. Tipton, *c.* 1908.)

STEVENS' KNOLL. Named for Captain Stevens' 5th Maine Battery, this rise of ground was the location from which a devastating artillery fire was poured into the attacking "Louisiana Tigers" on Cemetery Hill. This flanking fire, along with the arrival of reinforcements, contributed to the beating back of the Confederate attackers. (Leighton & Valentine, #216942; *c.* 1913.)

SPANGLER'S SPRING. Spangler's Spring, actually two springs, is located at the base of Culp's Hill. This source of cool, clean water was utilized by both armies. Union soldiers held possession of these waters until the evening of July 2, when the Confederates captured the springs and the nearby breastworks without a fight. On the morning of the last day of battle, Union troops recaptured the area. (Rotograph Co., #3701; 1904.)

GETTYSBURG, Pa. Spangler's Spring.

SPANGLER'S SPRING. Legend has it that the cooling waters of Spangler's Spring were shared peacefully by soldiers of both armies during the evening of July 2. However, no evidence exists to support this traditional story. The granite structure seen in this postcard was later constructed to enclose the spring. (Raphael Tuck & Sons, ser. #2397; c. 1907.)

Four

THE BATTLE DAY THREE
JULY 3, 1863

BATTLE OF GETTYSBURG, GETTYSBURG, PA.

BATTLE OF GETTYSBURG. The third day of this great battle saw its apex occur here at the center of the Union's defensive line. However, intense fighting was to take place in other areas of the battlefield as well. In this picture taken from the famous Cyclorama painting, we see Lieutenant Cushing's Battery in action at the Bloody Angle during Pickett's Charge. (David Kaufman, #102526; c. 1920.)

CULP'S HILL. Located on the right flank of the Union's defensive line (the "fish hook"), this was the scene of more fighting on the third day. During the night of July 2, General Greene's troops were reinforced by the remainder of the Union's 12th Corps. (W.H. Tipton, multiview set; *c.* 1905.)

CULP'S HILL. At about 4 a.m. Confederate forces under command of General Johnson once again attempted to dislodge the Union defenders. By 11 a.m. Union counter attacks successfully recaptured the breastworks and Spangler's Spring at the base of the hill. Confederate losses here were almost as great as those to be suffered during Pickett's Charge later in the day. (A.C. Bosselman & Co., #11716; *c.* 1910.)

Sprangler's Meadow, Gettysburg, Pa.

I would like to have by "by monday" P.

SPANGLER'S MEADOW. Located at the foot of Culp's Hill, this peaceful-looking meadow was the site of terrible bloodshed on the morning of July 3. Nearly 650 men of the 2nd Massachusetts and 27th Indiana Infantries attempted an ill-fated charge across this field. Upon reaching the edge of the woods, the Indiana Regiment managed to hold the position for only 10 minutes before having to retreat with over 40% casualties. (Rotograph Co., #3725; 1904.)

GETTYSBURG, PA

The House In whichJennieWad was killed and he Monument.

JENNIE WADE. On this morning (July 3), one of the most poignant incidents of the battle occurred. Twenty-year-old Miss Mary Virginia Wade (known as Jennie) was visiting her sister, Mrs. McClellen. While baking bread for her family and Union soldiers, a bullet believed to have been fired by a Confederate sniper passed through two doors, striking her in the back. She died instantly, becoming the only recorded civilian fatality of the battle. (Raphael Tuck & Sons, ser. #2397; c. 1907.)

SCENE ON CONFEDERATE AVENUE. Looking north from Pitzer's Woods along Confederate Avenue, cannons mark the position of Miller's Battery of the Washington Artillery from Louisiana. At 1 p.m. two guns from this battery fired in rapid succession to signal the start of the Confederates great cannonade against the Union line in preparation for Pickett's Charge. (David Kaufman, #102499; c. 1920.)

WEST CONFEDERATE AVENUE. Prior to Pickett's Charge, Colonel Alexander, who was in charge of Lee's artillery, began a fierce bombardment of the Union lines at 1 p.m. Nearly 150 Confederate cannon, many located here along West Confederate Avenue on Seminary Ridge, opened fire to be answered in return by 90 Union guns. This artillery duel would last nearly two hours. (Louis Kaufmann & Sons, #2; c. 1907.)

The Whitworth Battery.   Gettysburg, Pa.

WHITWORTH BATTERY. The Whitworth rifled cannon was a British-made breech loading fieldpiece. This gun was capable of firing a 12-pound shell called a "bolt" up to a distance of 5 miles. Shells from these guns could be distinguished from ordinary artillery by the distinctive whine they made in flight. The Confederates fielded two of these guns at Gettysburg while the Union had none. (American News Co., #A-6606; c. 1907.)

WEST CONFEDERATE AVENUE, SHOWING WHITWORTH GUNS, GETTYSBURG, PA.

WHITWORTH GUNS. Shown stationed along what is now West Confederate Avenue, these two Whitworth guns were part of the Confederate 3rd Corps battery known as Captain Hurt's Hardaway Artillery. On July 3 these two guns were moved to a safer location on Oak Hill, where they took part in the bombardment prior to Pickett's Charge. (C.T. Photochrom, #R-37854; c. 1913.)

PICKETT'S CHARGE, BATTLE OF GETTYSBURG, PA.

PICKETT'S CHARGE. Unsuccessful in breaking the Union lines on the left and right, General Lee believed that a massive attack on the center was necessary. Against the advice of General Longstreet, Lee ordered three divisions totaling approximately 15,000 men led by the Generals George Pickett, James Pettigrew, and Isaac Trimble to make the immortal assault. One of the most famous infantry charges in history, it was to result in Confederate forces suffering almost 10,000 casualties. Pickett's Charge, as it popularly became known, is shown in this painting by P.F. Rothermel. (C.T. Photochrom, #R-37829; c. 1913.)

Third Day's Battle-Pickett's Charge, Gettysburg, Pa.

PICKETT'S CHARGE. This picture depicting action during Pickett's Charge is the work of artist George Sacket and was first published in 1880. The Union 2nd Corps is shown defending the line while General Hancock courageously directs the troops from horseback. It was here at the stone wall that the Confederate assault was to climax. Some historians believe the failure of this attack marked the turning point of the entire Civil War. (J.I. Mumper; 1909.)

THE ANGLE. This key location, just to the right of the High Water Mark, received its name from the angle formed where two stone fences met. Behind this wall a battery of cannon commanded by Lt. Alonzo Cushing and infantry riflemen poured fire into the advancing rows of Confederates. (Louis Kaufmann & Sons, #40; c. 1907.)

Photo. only, Copyright 1904 by the Rotograph Co.
A 3713 The Bloody Angle, Gettysburg, Pa.

THE BLOODY ANGLE. It was at this spot that Confederate Gen. Lewis A. Armistead, his hat atop his sword, led 150 of his men over the stone wall of the "Angle." Armistead would fall, mortally wounded, as he reached the guns of Cushing's Battery. During hand-to-hand combat, most of his men were either killed or captured. (Rotograph Co., #A-3713; 1904.)

Death of Lieutenant Cushing at
Bloody Angle, Gettysburg, Pa.

DEATH OF LIEUTENANT CUSHING. Depicted in this picture is one of the most dramatic incidents of the third day's battle. The hero of the Bloody Angle, Lt. Alonzo Cushing was killed while firing his last functioning cannon directly into the advancing enemy as they were about to overrun his position. His brave sacrifice helped to break up the assault and turn the engagement into a Union victory. (A.C. Bosselman & Co., #13008; c. 1910.)

HANCOCK AVENUE. From this area, just behind the center of the Union defensive line, Federal infantry and artillery awaited the coming assault by Longstreet's Divisions. As the Confederate troops advanced, the gun batteries stationed here fired into their ranks inflicting heavy casualties. When the remnants of Pickett's Charge retreated, they left behind nearly two-thirds of their comrades dead, wounded, or captured. (Louis Kaufmann & Sons, #34; c. 1907.)

7229. HIGH WATER MARK, GETTYSBURG.　　　COPYRIGHT, 1903, BY DETROIT PHOTOGRAPHIC

HIGH WATER MARK. Here is seen the famous Copse of Trees, which served as the focal point of the Confederate attack on July 3. It was the intent of the Confederate infantry to converge on this very spot in hopes of breaking the center of the Union line. But it was here that the High Water Mark of the Confederacy is marked. (Detroit Photographic Co., #7229; 1903.)

EAST CAVALRY FIELD. Across farm fields, nearly 3 miles east of town, occurred the largest cavalry engagement of the battle. Confederate Gen. Jeb Stuart's 7,000 cavalrymen were to do combat with 5,000 Union horsemen. Stuart was attempting to turn the Union right flank and attack Meade from the rear. Charges and countercharges continued throughout the afternoon until the Confederate cavalry, low on ammunition and having suffered heavy losses, were forced to retreat. (Interstate News Co., #G-43; *c.* 1910.)

THE CAVALRY BATTLE. Illustrated here is a scene from the great cavalry battle that took place east of Gettysburg. In this incident Gen. Armstrong Custer, age 23, led the 1st Michigan Brigade in a charge against Gen. Wade Hampton's Brigade. Shouting "come on you wolverines," Custer inspired his men as they crashed into the Confederate ranks. The fighting became so violent that it has been referred to as "the saber fight." (J.I. Mumper; 1909.)

FARNSWORTH'S CHARGE. As one of the last actions of the battle of Gettysburg, Union Gen. Judson Kilpatrick ordered a cavalry attack against General Longstreet's right flank near Big Round Top. Despite objecting strenuously to his commander about the futility of his orders, Gen. Elon J. Farnsworth nevertheless led the 1st West Virginia Cavalry in the assault. After being struck by five bullets, Farnsworth would die fulfilling his duty. (M.A.P. Co., ser. 813; c. 1912.)

POTOMAC RIVER. After three days of battle, General Lee realized that the Union forces would not counterattack and began his retreat back to the South. Here at Williamsport, Maryland, the Army of Northern Virginia successfully withdrew across the Potomac River on July 14. Even though Gettysburg was to be General Lee's last offensive campaign, the war would continue for yet another two agonizing years. (Geo. W. Hurd; c. 1912.)

Five

HALLOWED GROUND
THE NATIONAL CEMETERY

SOLDIERS' NATIONAL CEMETERY. A few days after the battle, Pennsylvania Gov. A.G. Curtin appointed prominent attorney David Wills to begin the establishment of a cemetery. Wills selected 17 acres of ground at the highest point on Cemetery Hill to serve as the final resting place for those who fell in battle. This cemetery was to be the first in the United States dedicated exclusively to the burial of soldiers. (Albertype Co., c. 1900.)

Entrance to National Cemetery, Gettysburg, Pa.

ENTRANCE TO THE NATIONAL CEMETERY. Seen here is the eastern gate to the National Cemetery that opens onto Baltimore Pike. Dedicated on November 19, 1863, the cemetery was formally turned over to the federal government as a National Cemetery on May 1, 1872. An iron fence separates this burial ground from the neighboring civilian Evergreen Cemetery. (Rotograph Co., #3719; 1904.)

The Wills House, where Lincoln wrote his Gettysburg Address, Gettysburg, Pa.

WILLS HOUSE. Erected in 1814 at York Street and the square, this was the home of attorney David Wills. It was Wills who invited President Lincoln to come to Gettysburg for the dedication ceremonies of the National Cemetery. Lincoln put the finishing touches on his speech, the "Gettysburg Address," while staying here. (C.T. Photochrom, #R-37843; c. 1913.)

PRES. ABRAHAM LINCOLN. Born in 1809, Abraham Lincoln was elected the 16th President of the United States in 1860. Upon his election, a number of Southern states seceded from the union, thus bringing about the Civil War. Among the many things for which Lincoln is remembered is his immortal speech, the "Gettysburg Address." (J. Kuehler; c. 1908.)

COPYRIGHT, J. KOEHLER, N. Y.

ABRAHAM LINCOLN

LINCOLN DELIVERING HIS FAMOUS ADDRESS AT THE DEDICATION OF GETTYSBURG CEMETERY, NOV. 19, 1863.

LINCOLN DELIVERING HIS FAMOUS SPEECH. On November 19, 1863, Pres. Abraham Lincoln took part in the dedication ceremonies for the National Cemetery. Following a two-hour speech by famed orator Edward Everett, Lincoln rose to deliver his remarks, which lasted just over two minutes. Afterward, Lincoln was disappointed with his presentation and felt it to be inadequate. History, however, would prove otherwise. (M.W. Taggart, series #606; 1908.)

Gettysburg, Pa., 24 Jan 1907

Sent by Edmund J. Misany

Address delivered at the dedication of the Cemetery at Gettysburg.

Four score and seven years ago our fathers brought forth on this continent, a new nation, conceived in Liberty, and dedicated to the proposition that all men are created equal.

Now we are engaged in a great civil war, testing whether that nation, or any nation so conceived and so dedicated, can long endure. We are met on a great battle-field of that war. We have come to dedicate a portion of that field, as a final resting place for those who here gave their lives that that nation might live. It is altogether fitting and proper that we should do this.

But, in a larger sense, we can not dedicate---we can not consecrate---we can not hallow--this ground. The brave men, living and dead, who struggled here, have consecrated it, far above our poor power to add or detract. The world will little note, nor long remember what we say here, but it can never forget what they did here. It is for us the living, rather, to be dedicated here to the unfinished work which they who fought here have thus far so nobly advanced. It is rather for us to be dedicated to the great task remaining before us---that from these honored dead we take increased devotion to that cause for which they gave the last full measure of devotion---that we here highly resolve that these dead shall not have died in vain---that this nation, under God, shall have a new birth of freedom---and that government of the people, by the people, for the people, shall not perish from the earth.

Abraham Lincoln.

November 19, 1863.

LINCOLN'S "GETTYSBURG ADDRESS." Considered to be one of the finest speeches in our nation's history, the "Gettysburg Address" was penned five times by President Lincoln. The first copy is known as the Washington copy, while the second, the Wills copy, was completed in Gettysburg. In 1864 Lincoln wrote out three other drafts. It is the fifth, and only copy actually signed by Lincoln, that has become the standard version. Known as the Bliss copy, it now hangs in the Lincoln Room of the White House. (James T. Long; 1907.)

LINCOLN SPEECH MEMORIAL. Erected in 1912, this monument is dedicated to Abraham Lincoln's most famous speech. Having a semicircular form, its two bronze panels contain inscriptions of David Wills's invitation to Lincoln to speak at the dedication ceremonies and the words of the speech itself. Visitors to the cemetery can find this memorial inside the west gate entrance, to the right. (Interstate News Co., #G-41; c. 1916.)

ROSTRUM. From this ivy-covered platform near the west entrance to the cemetery, many dignitaries have addressed crowds gathered for memorial services. Memorial services have been an annual event since May 30, 1868. A number of our presidents, including Hayes, Cleveland, T. Roosevelt, and Wilson, as well as several others, have spoken here. (American News Co., #A-6610; c. 1907.)

IN THE SOLDIERS' NATIONAL CEMETERY. Shown here is one of the tree-lined walkways that pass through the cemetery. On the left is the civilian Evergreen Cemetery, while to the right is a section devoted to the battle's unknown dead. These pathways give visitors easy access to the grave sites of the fallen. (W.H. Tipton, #211; *c.* 1908.)

AVENUE IN NATIONAL CEMETERY. On this postcard from the early 1900s we see people on a leisurely stroll along one of the two tree-lined avenues running the length of the cemetery. The two cannon on the right mark the location of a Union artillery battery that was positioned here during the battle. One almost forgets that this peaceful locale was once the scene of combat. (Rotograph Co., #E-3701a; *c.* 1907.)

SOLDIERS' NATIONAL CEMETERY. Upon appointment by the governor of Pennsylvania, David Wills commissioned William Saunders, an eminent landscape gardener for the U.S. Department of Agriculture, to plan and design the layout of the cemetery. Each of the 18 Northern states that took part in the battle contributed to the costs. (W.H. Tipton, #S-651; 1906.)

NATIONAL CEMETERY. Once the cemetery was established, the remains of over 3,500 Union dead were interred here. Between 1870 and 1873 some 3,320 Confederate dead originally buried here were transferred to Southern cemeteries. There are presently over 7,000 interments in the cemetery as veterans of later wars are now buried here within separate areas. (J.I. Mumper; 1909.)

SOLDIERS' NATIONAL CEMETERY. When William Saunders designed the cemetery, he laid out the burial plots in a semicircular fashion with the dead arranged in parallel rows. There are 22 different sections. Each of the 18 Union states was assigned its own area; one section was reserved for U.S. Regular Army dead and three sections were devoted to the graves of the unknown. (Hugh C. Leighton, #5697; c. 1908.)

Graves of the Unknown Dead in The Soldiers' National Cemetery, Gettysburg, Pa.

GRAVES OF THE UNKNOWN. Great care was taken to identify the bodies of the dead when they were removed from the battlefield and during reinterment. However, due to the nature of the fighting and the identification techniques of the time, many remained unidentifiable. Today 1,664 bodies of those who fell in battle remain unnamed. (Excelsior, #B-4588; *c.* 1910.)

"Unknown Dead"

Gettysburg, Pa..

UNKNOWN DEAD. Of the 1,664 unknown dead, some 979 remain unidentifiable even as to their state military unit. In this real photo postcard we see the rows of small, uniformly sized stone markers that record the final resting place for these fallen warriors. (Real photo card; *c.* 1904.)

NEW YORK STATE MONUMENT. This monument, located within the cemetery, stands 93 feet tall and is among the tallest at Gettysburg. Erected in 1893, it overlooks the 867 burial plots devoted to the dead from New York state. New York troops suffered the highest number of casualties of any of the Union states during the battle. (A.C. Bosselman & Co., #2382; c. 1910.)

SOLDIERS' NATIONAL MONUMENT. Standing near the spot where Lincoln gave his famous address, this monument was the first memorial of any kind to be placed at Gettysburg. The cornerstone for this monument was laid on July 4, 1865. Gen. George G. Meade, "the Victor of Gettysburg," was among the dignitaries who spoke at the dedication ceremonies on July 1, 1869. (Union News Co., #1155; c. 1910.)

GETTYSBURG, Pa. Soldiers National Monument. - National Cemetery.

SOLDIERS' NATIONAL MONUMENT. Positioned at the center of the semicircle of gravesites, this monument stands as a tribute to all who fought here. Standing 60 feet high, its 25-foot-square pedestal accommodates four marble statues. The statues sculpted by Randolph Rogers, symbolize "War," "History," "Peace," and "Plenty," while the statue on top is the "Genius of Liberty." (Raphael Tuck & Sons, ser. #2397; c. 1907.)

GENERAL COLLIS MONUMENT. In memory of Gen. Charles H.T. Collis, this memorial is situated near to the Soldiers' Monument. At the start of the war Collis organized a company of Zouaves, which later became Co. A of the 114th Pennsylvania Volunteer Infantry, also commonly called "Collis' Zouaves." This unit was to take part in many campaigns of the war and unlike most other Zouave companies, they maintained their distinctive uniforms throughout the conflict. (Pub. unknown; c. 1906.)

GEN. JOHN F. REYNOLDS MONUMENT. Honoring Gen. John F. Reynolds, a native son of Pennsylvania, this was the first portrait statue erected at Gettysburg. Dedicated August 31, 1872, it was sculpted by J.Q.A. Ward from a photograph of the general. Originally intended to be placed at the site of his death, it was ultimately placed near the east entrance to the cemetery. (Rotograph Co., #3710; 1904.)

A 3702 Jennie Wade's Monument, Gettysburg, Pa

I love this card

Roscoe

JENNIE WADE MONUMENT. The only civilian from Gettysburg to be killed during the battle, Jenny Wade is buried not in the National Cemetery but in the adjoining public Evergreen Cemetery. Her gravesite is marked by a pedestaled statue that was dedicated on September 16, 1901. In 1910 a flagpole was placed alongside her monument and a law passed allowing a flag to be flown both day and night in her honor. (Rotograph Co., #A-3702; 1904.)

Six

In Remembrance
Monuments and Memorials

Monuments at Gettysburg. In May of 1879 a small granite memorial to honor the men of the 2nd Massachusetts Infantry Regiment was dedicated. Since then, nearly 1,400 monuments, memorials, markers, and tablets have been placed around the battlefield to pay tribute to those who fought here. This real photo postcard catches the images of three such remembrances. (Real photo card; 1907.)

ETTYSBURG, Pa.   Statues of Generals Hancock, Meade and Reynolds.

This is very cool weather. Daniel C. G

EQUESTRIAN STATUES. Among the most impressive memorials on the battlefield are the equestrian statues. These bronze sculptures stand in tribute to the significant military commanders. At Gettysburg, traditionally the position of the horses' feet indicated the fate of the rider during the battle. If both feet are raised, the rider was killed in action; if one hoof is lifted, he was wounded; and if both feet are planted on the ground, he survived unscathed. This unwritten custom ended in 1998 with the erection of a statue honoring General Longstreet. (Raphael Tuck & Sons, ser. #2397; c. 1907.)

BUFORD, REYNOLDS, AND HALL MONUMENTS. Standing on the spot of the opening of the battle on July 1, the statues of Generals Buford and Reynolds face the positions of General Heth's advancing army. The monument on the right honors Hall's Maine Battery of the 1st Corps, which helped support Union forces on the first day of battle. (Louis Kaufmann & Sons, #19; c. 1907.)

GENERAL REYNOLDS MONUMENT. Considered by many to have been one of the Union's most capable commanders, Gen. John F. Reynolds was the first general to fall in battle at Gettysburg. The work of sculptor Henry K. Bush-Brown, this statue is located just several hundred yards north of the spot where he was killed on July 1. (Louis Kaufmann & Sons, #18; c. 1907.)

75

MCPHERSON BARN. Here at the McPherson Barn, along the Chambersburg Pike (Route 30), stands a figural monument immortalizing the 149th Pennsylvania Infantry Regiment, also known as the "Pennsylvania Bucktails Brigade." On the right is a memorial dedicated to Battery A of the 2nd U.S. Artillery, also called Calef's Battery, whose six rifled cannon fought here on July 1, until relieved by Hall's Maine Battery. (Leighton & Valentine, #216938; *c.* 1913.)

JOHN L. BURNS STATUE. John Burns, the "Hero of Gettysburg" and the only citizen known to have fought in the battle, is honored with this statue situated close to the McPherson Barn on Stone Avenue. The bronze likeness of Burns is mounted upon a pedestal of native rock near the spot where he joined the 150th Pennsylvania Infantry Regiment on the first day of battle. (A.C. Bosselman & Co., #11721; *c.* 1910.)

SCENE ON REYNOLDS AVENUE. Situated on Reynolds Avenue is the bronze tribute to Gen. Abner Doubleday. Doubleday took over command of the 1st Corps when General Reynolds was killed in action. The Union soldiers held their ground here just west of Gettysburg until overwhelmed by increasing numbers of the enemy. General Doubleday was later relieved from temporary command after his troops retreated from their positions. (David Kaufman, #102502; c. 1920.)

SCENE ON REYNOLDS AVENUE. This view shows several of the monuments that have been placed along Reynolds Avenue. In the center is the standing bronze figure of Gen. James Wadsworth, commander of the first Union infantry division. To the right of this statue is a monument to the 147th New York Infantry, and on the far right, an obelisk honoring the 3rd Indiana Cavalry. (David Kaufman, #102515; c. 1920.)

TWENTY-SIXTH PENNSYLVANIA EMERGENCY REGIMENT MONUMENT. Located at the junction of Buford and Springs Avenues, this statue immortalizes the 26th Pennsylvania Emergency Militia Regiment. Hastily assembled, this untrained unit of volunteers (which included one company composed of local college and seminary students) was no match for the battle-hardened Confederate army. (Hugh C. Leighton, #4750; c. 1908.)

EAST CEMETERY HILL. After the death of General Reynolds on July 1, General Meade sent Gen. Winfield S. Hancock to assume command of the Union forces. At the top of East Cemetery Hill stands an equestrian statue of General Hancock. This has been placed where the general rallied his troops and directed the establishment of his defensive lines on July 1. (W.H. Tipton; c. 1911.)

78

CAVALRY MONUMENT. This granite monument honoring members of the 17th Pennsylvania Cavalry is located near the intersection of Buford Avenue and the Mummasburg Road. Dedicated September 11, 1889, the memorial is in the form of a bas relief and shows a life-sized mounted trooper in the role of the "eyes of the army." (Rotograph Co., #E-3708a; c. 1907.)

GEN. GEORGE G. MEADE MONUMENT. Meade's monument stands along Hancock Avenue at a spot close to where he stood on July 3, 1863, observing the retreat of Pickett's Charge. The statue, sculpted by Henry K. Bush-Brown, depicts General Meade hatless, just as he looked on the day his Union army celebrated victory. (Union News Co., #1136; c. 1910.)

BORN DECEMBER 31, 1815

DIED NOVEMBER 6, 1872

GEN. GEORGE G. MEADE. A graduate of the West Point class of 1835, Gen. George G. Meade was appointed by President Lincoln to command the Army of the Potomac only a few days prior to the battle. Remembered as the "Victor of Gettysburg," he is portrayed mounted upon his horse "Baldy." The horse was seriously wounded during the battle but survived to be a part of the general's funeral cortege in 1872. (A.C. Bosselman & Co., #2380; c. 1910.)

FORTY-FOURTH AND TWELFTH NEW YORK INFANTRY MONUMENT. Honoring the men and officers of the 44th New York Infantry and two companies of the 12th New York Infantry, this structure stands 44 feet tall, the largest regimental monument on the battlefield. Designed by David Butterfield, a former commander of the unit, its unique granite castle form incorporates an observation deck, allowing visitors to view the valley below. (Rotograph Co., #E-3700b; c. 1907.)

TWELFTH AND FORTY-FOURTH NEW YORK INFANTRY MONUMENT. This imposing monument to the 12th and 44th New York Infantry Regiments stands approximately 100 feet behind the positions held by these two units from about 5 p.m. on July 2 to about 11 a.m. on July 3, 1863. Inside the building, bronze plaques list the names of all those who served in these regiments. Another feature are two bas reliefs of their commanding officers, Gen. Francis Barlow and Gen. Daniel Butterfield. (David Kaufman, #102513; c. 1920.)

81

SUMMIT OF LITTLE ROUND TOP. Gen. Gouverneur K. Warren, the "Savior of Little Round Top," is memorialized by this bronze statue, which stands forever gazing out from the summit of Little Round Top. As chief engineer of the Army of the Potomac, it was his timely decision to order the occupying of the heights of Little Round Top that saved this vital position for the Union army. (J.I. Mumper; 1909.)

SCENE FROM LITTLE ROUND TOP. On the summit of Little Round Top stands the monument to the 155th Pennsylvania Infantry. The granite, life-size statue of a Zouave in his distinctive uniform faces the valley below. It was from this location that the troops watched and waited to defend the heights on July 2 and 3. The road shown here no longer exists. (David Blocher, #102498; c. 1920.)

FOURTH NEW YORK INDEPENDENT MONUMENT. Located along Sickles Avenue, just above Devil's Den, this monument pays tribute to the artillerymen of the 4th New York Battery. Also known as Smith's Battery, they were part of Gen. Daniel Sickles's 3rd Corps. This unit saw heavy action on July 2, when they were forced to withdraw from this spot with a loss of three of their four cannon. (Louis Kaufman & Sons, #28; c. 1907.)

WHEAT FIELD, GETTYSBURG. PA.

THE WHEATFIELD. Along DeTrobriand Avenue, location of "The Wheatfield," are numerous memorials. On the right is a monument to the 17th Maine, which is formed by a pedestal topped with the figure of a soldier behind a stone wall. This commemorates the tenacious defense made by the men of this regiment. To the left is a memorial to the 115th Pennsylvania Infantry. (David Kaufman, #102518; c. 1920.)

THE WHEATFIELD. This view, taken along Ayres Avenue north of Devil's Den, shows part of the area known as The Wheatfield. To the left is a monument for the 148th Pennsylvania Infantry; memorials to other regiments dot the field. The number of markers gives evidence to the fact that this was an area that saw considerable combat. (J.I. Mumper; 1909.)

PENNSYLVANIA RESERVE LINE IN WHEATFIELD. Positioned along Ayres Avenue at the edge of the Wheatfield are monuments to several regiments that helped to support General Sickles' extended line. From left to right are the memorials to the 11th, 1st, and 2nd Pennsylvania Reserve Regiments, which were part of the Union 5th Corps sent to assist General Sickles. (Louis Kaufmann & Sons, #31; c. 1907.)

GETTYSBURG, Pa. Irish Brigade Monument in Wheat Field Woods.
63d, 69th, 88th N. Y. Infantry.

IRISH BRIGADE MONUMENT. The "Irish Brigade," commanded by Col. Patrick Kelly, formed the 2nd Brigade of the 1st Division of Hancock's Corps. This memorial honors the bravery with which this unit fought on July 2. The large, granite Celtic cross is located in a wooded area just west of The Wheatfield, where they did battle. At the base of the monument is a life-size, bronze Irish wolf hound, which is a symbol of faith and devotion. (Raphael Tuck & Sons, ser. #2397; c. 1907.)

IRISH BRIGADE MONUMENT, FATHER CORBY STATUE.

IRISH BRIGADE MONUMENT, FATHER CORBY STATUE. This postcard shows two related monuments. On the left is the "Irish Brigade" memorial and on the right is the statue of Father William Corby, chaplain of the brigade. Father Corby stood upon this very rock and delivered an inspirational talk to the troops before granting them absolution only moments prior to their being sent into battle. After the war, Father Corby would become president of Notre Dame University. (C.T. Photochrom, #R-37830; c. 1913.)

Irish Brigade Memorial
Catholic Church, Gettysburg, Pa.

IRISH BRIGADE MEMORIAL. Another memorial to the all "Irish Brigade" can be found in St. Francis Xavier Catholic Church on West High Street in Gettysburg. The church, built in 1852, served as a hospital from the first day of battle, and Confederate Gen. Richard Ewell was to use it for observation purposes on July 2. (Gettysburg Compiler; c. 1910.)

FIRST MASSACHUSETTS MONUMENT. This beautifully carved memorial to the 1st Massachusetts Infantry is in recognition of their contribution to helping hold the advanced Union positions on July 2. The memorial is situated just north of Sickles Avenue, along the Emmitsburg Road. (W.H. Tipton, multiview set; *c.* 1905.)

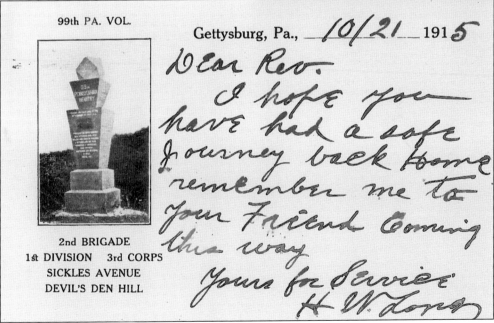

99th PA. VOL.

2nd BRIGADE
1st DIVISION   3rd CORPS
SICKLES AVENUE
DEVIL'S DEN HILL

Gettysburg, Pa., 10/21 1915

Dear Rev.
I hope you have had a safe journey back home remember me to your friend coming this way
Yours for Service
H. W. Long

NINETY-NINTH PENNSYLVANIA VOLUNTEER MONUMENT. As part of the Union 3rd Corps, the 99th Pennsylvania Regiment took part in General Sickles' controversial deployment of his men forward of the Union lines. The 99th Regiment was positioned near the summit of Devil's Den, and it is on top of this famous battlefield landmark that their monument stands today. (Typographical Union Label; *c.* 1915.)

GETTYSBURG, Pa.   Gen. Robert E. Lee,
his Headquarters and two Confederate Monuments.

TWO CONFEDERATE MONUMENTS. Here are two of the earliest memorials dedicated to elements of the Confederate army. In the upper-left corner is the memorial that marks the spot at the "Bloody Angle," where Gen. Lewis Armistead was mortally wounded on July 3. On the right is the monument to the 2nd Maryland Infantry, and Lee's headquarters is pictured below his portrait. (Raphael Tuck & Sons, ser. #2397; c. 1907.)

CONFEDERATE TABLETS ON CONFEDERATE AVENUE, SEMINARY RIDGE, GETTYSBURG, PA

CONFEDERATE TABLETS ON CONFEDERATE AVENUE. This row of memorial tablets runs along one side of Confederate Avenue. They were placed here to honor the valor of the Confederate troops who occupied and held this area of Seminary Ridge during the entire three days' battle. A similar set of tablets can be found on Cemetery Hill, honoring Union troops. (Leighton & Valentine, #216936; c. 1913.)

SECOND MARYLAND CONFEDERATE MONUMENT. The first Confederate monument to be erected on the battlefield is situated at the base of Culp's Hill. It was here that the 2nd Maryland Infantry successfully assaulted and captured the Union defenses on July 2; however, they were to be driven out on July 3. This memorial was dedicated on November 19, 1886. A second, smaller marker was placed about 100 yards farther up the hill to indicate the position they reached during the July 3rd fighting. (Louis Kaufman & Sons, #3; c. 1907.)

GENERAL SLOCUM'S STATUE AND STEVENS KNOLL. On top of the hill to the left is a monument to the 5th Maine Artillery. This battery was commanded by Capt. Grenleaf T. Stevens, for whom this small rise of ground is named. It was fire from the six cannon of this battery that helped drive back the Confederates assaulting the hill on July 2. To the right is the statue of Gen. Henry Slocum. (J.I. Mumper; 1909.)

GEN. H.W. SLOCUM. The equestrian statue of Gen. Henry W. Slocum, commander of the Union's 12th Corps, was erected by the State of New York (his homeland) atop Stevens Knoll. When meeting with other commanders at General Meade's headquarters on the evening of July 2, his famous phrase, "Stay and fight it out!" expressed the unanimous decision of the officers present; it also resulted in the battle continuing for a third day. (W.H. Tipton; c. 1906.)

GENERAL GREENE'S STATUE. This portrait statue stands in honor of Gen. George S. Greene, the commander of 1,350 New York troops on the summit of Culp's Hill. At the age of 62, Greene was the oldest field commander in the Army of the Potomac. This postcard, showing his bronze statue, was postmarked October 1, only five days after the statue's dedication on September 26, 1907. (Pub. unknown; 1907.)

SUMMIT OF CULP'S HILL. General Greene's statue looks out over the hill where his New York Brigade, outnumbered three to one, defended Culp's Hill on the evening of July 2. To the left is one of the five observation towers erected on the battlefield for visitor use. On the right is a small monument to the 1st Pennsylvania Artillery. (J.I. Mumper; 1909.)

SUMMIT OF CULP'S HILL. Here is shown a closer view of the granite memorial to members of the 1st Pennsylvania Artillery, also known as Knap's Battery, which was commanded by Lt. Charles A. Atwell. The memorial is situated on the north side of Culp's Hill, and it was from here that the battery, after having cleared gaps in the trees through which to fire, fought an artillery duel with the Confederates. (Detroit Photographic Co., #8377, 1903.)

SECOND BRIGADE MONUMENT. Standing just over 23 feet tall and representing a "tower of invincible strength," this monument stands atop Culp's Hill. Part of General Slocum's 12th Corps, the 150th New York Infantry helped to defend this location against Confederate attack and was honored with this granite tower. (David Kaufman, #102497, c. 1920.)

THE WEST VIRGINIA INFANTRY MONUMENT. East Cemetery Hill, the scene of heavy combat, is marked with many memorials. Shown in the right foreground is the granite statue dedicated to the soldiers of the 7th West Virginia Infantry Regiment. The back of the monument's pedestal is inscribed with the slogan "Sons of the Mountains." To the left is a tribute to the 73rd Pennsylvania Infantry, which in hand-to-hand fighting helped repel the enemy from the summit. (Union News Co., #1156; c. 1910.)

EAST CEMETERY HILL. Another view of East Cemetery Hill shows General Hancock's statue (left), a monument to the 1st Pennsylvania Artillery Battery B (center) and a memorial to the 4th Ohio Infantry (right). The 4th Ohio helped push back the attack by Hay's and Hoke's Confederate Brigades early on the evening of July 2. This monument stands just over 28 feet tall and is topped by a white bronze statue of a soldier at parade rest. (David Blocher, #129677; c. 1920.)

GENERAL HANCOCK. This large, bronze equestrian statue honors Gen. Winfield S. Hancock. As commander of the Union 2nd Corps, he was wounded in the thigh while directing his troops at the center of the defensive line on July 3. He survived the battle and in 1880 ran as the Democratic candidate for president but was narrowly defeated by James Garfield. (Louis Kaufman & Sons, #16; c. 1907.)

WRIGHT AVENUE. Erected along the edge of Wright Avenue, which is on the southern end of the battlefield, is a large granite figure of a resting lion. This monument honors the men of Gen. Lewis A. Grant's Brigade of the 6th Corps. These troops, which hailed from Vermont, were stationed here in reserve during the first and second day of the battle. (Hugh C. Leighton, #4745, c. 1908.)

SLOCUM AVENUE. Situated along South Slocum Avenue, the site of fierce combat over two days, is a regimental monument for the 123rd New York Infantry Regiment. Part of General Slocum's 12th Corps, this unit was involved in the recapture of the breastworks during the morning of July 3. This artistic memorial is topped by the statue of Clio, the Greek goddess of history. She is portrayed in the act of recording the events of the battle. (W.H. Tipton, #206; c. 1908.)

MINNESOTA AND PENNSYLVANIA MONUMENTS. Close to the Pennsylvania monument on Hancock Avenue is the memorial to the 1st Minnesota Infantry Regiment. It stands on the spot from which the regiment launched a gallant counterattack against Wilcox's Confederate Brigade on the evening of July 2. In successfully saving the Union line, the Regiment would suffer over 82% casualties, all killed or wounded. (David Kaufman, #102506; c. 1902.)

SPANGLER'S MEADOW. On the edge of Spangler's Meadow is a small granite marker placed in memory of the men of the 2nd Massachusetts Infantry. It was here that some 316 men of the regiment made a courageous but unsuccessful charge across the field. Dedicated in May of 1879, this was the first regimental monument of any kind on the battlefield. On the back of the memorial is a plaque listing the names of all 45 men from the unit who died in the engagement. (Louis Kaufman & Sons, #12; c. 1907.)

NEW YORK MONUMENT. This granite memorial commemorates the 126th New York Infantry Regiment, part of the 3rd Division of Hancock's 2nd Corps. They took part in holding the defensive line against the massive Confederate assault on the Union center July 3. The monument is placed in Zeiglers Grove, very near the Cyclorama building. (Union News Co., #1162; c. 1910.)

FIRST NEW YORK LIGHT ARTILLERY MONUMENT. Located along Hancock Avenue, the memorial in the foreground pays tribute to the members of Capt. Robert H. Fitzhugh's Battery K, 1st New York Artillery. During the great artillery bombardment preceding Pickett's Charge, this battery served as a replacement unit for those guns damaged by enemy fire. They were to be engaged during the remainder of the action that day. (David Kaufman, #102514; c. 1920.)

NEW YORK MONUMENT. Along North Hancock Avenue, near the Brian Barn, stands the bronze figure of a Union infantry skirmisher. Part of the 2nd Corps, the 111th New York Infantry commanded by Col. George Willard were to serve as skirmishers throughout the battle. This monument, dedicated June 26, 1891, stands on the spot where the regimental colors stood during Pickett's Charge. (Union News Co., #1153; *c.* 1910.)

THE BLOODY ANGLE. Located on Webb Avenue at the Angle, this memorial pays tribute to the 72nd Pennsylvania Infantry known also as the "Philadelphia Fire Zouaves." This regiment rushed in to oppose Armistead and his men as they surged over the stone wall at the Angle. The monument's placement was marked by controversy. It finally took a decision by the Pennsylvania Supreme Court to settle the issue. (Cunningham & Co.; *c.* 1915.)

U.S. Regulars Monument. Located near the High Water Mark on Hancock Avenue, this impressive monument honors units of the Regular U.S. Army who fought here. Although greatly outnumbered by the volunteer units, these professional soldiers greatly contributed to the outcome of the battle. They were to be engaged over all areas of the battlefield and took part in some of the bloodiest of the fighting. (Union News Co., #1130; c. 1910.)

U.S. Regulars Monument. Standing 85 feet tall, this granite obelisk was dedicated on May 30, 1909, by Pres. William Howard Taft before a large assemblage of members of the U.S. Regular Army. Around the base of the monument are four large plaques listing each of the regiments and their commanders who fought at Gettysburg. An unusual feature of this memorial is the large patio that allows visitors to walk around the pedestal. (W.H. Tipton; 1909.)

TAMMANY MONUMENT. Known as the Tammany Regiment and nicknamed the "Braves," this memorial honors the members of the 42nd New York Infantry who helped repel Pickett's Charge. Situated along Hancock Avenue, the granite base is topped by the bronze statue of Chief Tamenend, a former Delaware Indian chief. This very unusual monument was dedicated on September 24, 1891. (American News Co., #A6607; c. 1907.)

STATE OF VERMONT MONUMENT. The tall column in the center of this view is the Vermont State Monument. Located on Hancock Avenue, it marks the point from which Gen. George J. Stannard's Vermont Brigade launched its counterattack against Pickett's flank, helping to halt the Confederate advance. (Union News Co., #1154; c. 1910.)

MONUMENT OF FIRST VERMONT BRIGADE. Dedicated on October 9, 1889, this 55-foot-high granite column stands as a tribute to all four of the Vermont units that fought at Gettysburg. On top of the fluted column stands an 11-foot-tall bronze likeness of Gen. George J. Stannard. At the base are inscriptions describing the services performed by these Vermont regiments. (Rotograph Co., #3716; 1904.)

Monument of First Vermont Brigade, Gettysburg, Pa.

VIRGINIA STATE MEMORIAL. Virginia's memorial to her native sons is an impressive monument topped by the statue of Gen. Robert E. Lee astride his favorite horse "Traveller." This equestrian statue of Lee is said to rank among the finest in the world. At the base of the memorial stand seven figures representing the various branches of the Army of Northern Virginia. Located on West Confederate Avenue, it overlooks the scene of Pickett's Charge. (Louis Kaufmann & Sons; c. 1917.)

SCENE ON HANCOCK AVENUE. Standing on the granite pedestal is a bronze likeness of Gen. Alexander S. Webb. A Congressional Medal of Honor winner, Webb commanded a Philadelphia Brigade here at the focal point of Pickett's Charge. On the right is a memorial to the 1st Pennsylvania Cavalry, which had been held in reserve in case of a Confederate breakthrough. The life-size bronze statue depicts a dismounted cavalryman ready to do battle. (David Kaufman, #102501; c. 1920.)

EIGHTH PENNSYLVANIA CAVALRY MONUMENT. A fine-looking granite sculpture of a horse and rider pays tribute to troopers of the Eighth Pennsylvania Cavalry Regiment. These soldiers, commanded by Capt. William A. Corrie, were part of several cavalry units that made up the Union line on Cemetery Ridge on July 2 and 3. This monument stands in the shadow of the Pennsylvania State Memorial. (David Kaufman, #102505; *c.* 1920.)

AT THE HIGH WATER MARK. Here at the High Water Mark can be found one of three tributes devoted to the 106th Pennsylvania Infantry Regiment. This regiment was involved in heavy fighting at several locations on July 2 and 3. This monument was dedicated in 1889. It is topped by three carved-granite drums forming the trefoil symbol of the Union 2nd Corps of which they were a part. (C.A. Blocher, multiview set; *c.* 1905.)

103

High Water Mark, Gettysburg. Reached by Reading "fast trains.

HIGH WATER MARK MONUMENT. Located at the famed Copse of Trees, along Hancock Avenue, this memorial marks the site of the High Water Mark of the Confederacy. It was here that the assault by Pickett's, Pettigrew's, and Trimble's Divisions on July 3 reached its zenith. (Pub. unknown, *c.* 1900.)

CLOSE UP OF HIGH WATER MARK, GETTYSBURG, PA.

HIGH WATER MARK MONUMENT. The monument at the High Water Mark is in the form of a huge, open book that is propped up by pyramids of cannonballs. Upon the pages are inscribed the names of the various Confederate and Union forces that faced each other in deadly combat on that fateful afternoon. (David Kaufman, #102509; *c.* 1920.)

Pennsylvania State Memorial, Gettysburg, Pa.

PENNSYLVANIA STATE MEMORIAL. The largest and most impressive of the state memorials, the Pennsylvania Memorial on Hancock Avenue honors the 34,530 soldiers from the commonwealth who fought here. The largest contingent of Union forces at Gettysburg, the names of each individual from Pennsylvania is recorded on bronze tablets placed around the parapets and on the inner walls of the arches. (A.C. Bosselman & Co., #11737; c. 1910.)

105

PENNSYLVANIA STATE MEMORIAL. The Pennsylvania Memorial was constructed in the form of a massive dome supported by four large arches standing on a parapet 84 feet square. On top of the dome stands a 21-foot-tall statue of the "Goddess of Victory and Peace" that was cast from the bronze of cannon actually used during the Civil War. (Real photo card; c. 1910.)

STATUE OF GEN. WM. WELLS. 1ST. VERMONT CAVALRY, GETTYSBURG, PA.

STATUE OF GENERAL WILLIAM WELLS. On South Confederate Avenue stands the monument to the 1st Vermont Cavalry and their commander, Maj. William Wells. Four companies of this cavalry unit accompanied Gen. Elon J. Farnsworth during his futile and fatal charge against Law's Alabama Brigade at 5 p.m. on July 3. For his part in this, the final encounter of the Battle of Gettysburg, Major Wells received the Congressional Medal of Honor. (W.H. Tipton; c. 1913.)

Seven

THE LATER YEARS
VETERANS AND VISITORS

BATTLE OF GETTYSBURG FIELD. On April 30, 1884, the Gettysburg Battlefield Memorial Association was established by the Commonwealth of Pennsylvania to purchase portions of the battlefield and preserve it for future generations. An act of Congress in 1895 placed the park under the jurisdiction of the U.S. War Department until 1933, when it was transferred to the National Parks Service. Thus the Gettysburg National Military Park was brought into existence. (Koelling & Klappenbach, #59; c. 1904.)

WEST CONFEDERATE AVE., GETTYSBURG, PA.

WEST CONFEDERATE AVENUE. As the Battlefield Park was developed, more sections of the battlefield were purchased. Sites for regimental monuments and the various memorials were selected and the different lines of battle surveyed and accurately marked. To make the field of battle more accessible to visitors, miles of roads and avenues were developed. One of the first roads to be paved was Confederate Avenue. (Rotograph Co., #E-3703a; c. 1907.)

ROUND TOP FROM CONFEDERATE AVE., GETTYSBURG, PA.

ROUNDTOP, FROM CONFEDERATE AVENUE. When the battlefield was transferred to the federal government in 1895, there were 17 miles of roads. By 1933 a total of 26 miles of paved avenues allowed visitors to travel around the battlegrounds. Today there are approximately 40 miles of paved roadway in the Gettysburg National Military Park. (Rotograph Co., #E-3702a; c. 1907.)

ETTYSBURG, Pa. West Confederate Avenue, Looking North.

WEST CONFEDERATE AVENUE. During the early 1900s, visitors often toured the battlefield by wagon or horse cart, as seen in this postcard view. It was from this location (on what is now West Confederate Avenue) that Confederate artillery bombarded Union positions for nearly two hours prior to Pickett's Charge. (Raphael Tuck & Sons, ser. #2397; c. 1907.)

East Confederate Avenue. Gettysburg, Pa.

EAST CONFEDERATE AVENUE. Positioned on the eastern side of the battlefield, East Confederate Avenue follows the contours of the land and curves behind Culp's Hill. One of the earliest roads constructed on the battlefield, it still exists, unlike the many others that have been changed or removed over the years. It is one of the more scenic but less traveled roads. (Excelsior, #A1891; c. 1910.)

Sykes Avenue on Little Round Top, Gettysburg, Pa.

SYKES AVENUE. At the time of the battle, Little Round Top was a roadless hill. On the afternoon of July 2, Lieutenant Hazlett's artillery battery and Col. Strong Vincent's Brigade found the climb to the top an arduous task. Today tourists find that the paved road known as Sykes Avenue provides easy access to this important site. Note the tree in the foreground, which, despite severe damage from a Confederate artillery shell, continued to live and grow for many years. (W.H. Tipton, #311; c. 1910.)

SUMMIT OF CULP'S HILL. In 1895 the government erected five steel observation towers at strategic points on the battlefield. This allowed tourists to look out over large areas where the conflict occurred. Several of the towers have been removed over the years, and today only two and a half still remain. One of those still in use is this tower, located atop the summit of Culp's Hill. (A.C. Bosselman & Co., #11722; *c.* 1910.)

OBSERVATION TOWER ON OAK RIDGE. Located at the northern end of the battlefield, this observation tower offered a birds-eye view of various sections of the battleground. Today only one-half of this tower still stands. To the left of the tower is the unusual, granite "oak tree-shaped" monument to the 90th Pennsylvania Infantry Regiment. (Leighton & Valentine, #216930; *c.* 1913.)

111

OBSERVATION TOWER ON CONFEDERATE AVENUE. Located on Confederate Avenue, this observation tower gives visitors a view from the position of the Southern forces during much of the battle. The five towers, which were erected expressly for sightseeing purposes, cost the government $50,000 to install. (David Blocher, #129675; c. 1920.)

GETTYSBURG, Pa, View from Tower on Hancock Avenue.

VIEW FROM THE TOWER ON HANCOCK AVENUE. A visitor could get an excellent panoramic view of the battlefield from atop the tower on Hancock Avenue. This postcard view shows much of the second and third days' battlefield as it appeared in the early 1900s. The tower from which this picture was taken no longer stands. (Raphael Tuck & Sons, ser. # 2397; c. 1907.)

FIFTIETH ANNIVERSARY. After the war the veterans of this great conflict were to return for three major reunions. The first was in 1888, a little before the age of the postcard. The 50th reunion, which lasted from June 29 to July 6, 1913, saw an estimated 55,000 veterans attend the activities. The final reunion was in 1938, when 1,845 visited the battlefield. At that time the average age of a veteran was 94 years. (Howard Keyser; 1913.)

Gov. Felker and Drum Corps at Gettysburg, July 1 to 4, 1913.

GOVERNOR FELKER AND DRUM CORPS. Here is a group of New York G.A.R. (Grand Army of the Republic) veterans at their campsite during the 50th reunion. Most of the thousands of returning ex-soldiers camped on the old battlegrounds. The former combatants of both North and South met in peace and remembrance of those history-making days a half century earlier. (Real photo card; 1913.)

MARY TEBE The Vivandere with Collis' Zouavas (114th Penna.)at Gettysburg, Pa.

Copyright 1908 by W. H. Tipton.

MARY TEBE. One of the most unusual veterans of the battle was Mary Tebe, nicknamed "French Mary," who served the 114th Pennsylvania Infantry (Collis's Zouaves) as a vivandere. A vivandere was a combination of nurse, cook, seamstress, and laundress. For her duties, Mary drew a soldier's pay and is considered to have been the only enlisted woman at Gettysburg. She carried water and treated the wounded during the heaviest of the fighting and was beloved by her unit. In this photo she had just returned to the battlefield for a visit. (W.H. Tipton, #201; 1908.)

TOUR BY WAGON. Visitors have toured the battlefield park by various means over the years. Here is a group of sightseers traveling by horse-drawn wagon through a wooded section of the battlefield sometime during the early 1900s. This would have been a very pleasant means of traveling over the battlegrounds in those early days. (Real photo card; *c.* 1905.)

TOUR GROUP ON LITTLE ROUND TOP. On this real photo postcard, we see what appears to be an early tour group posing atop Little Round Top with General Warren's statue behind them. Their "guide" (standing to the left) is possibly a veteran of the battle, as were many of the early guides. (Real photo card; *c.* 1908.)

FIRST DAY'S FIELD. Capt. James T. Long, a veteran of the battle, is shown leading an automobile tour of the battlefield. He is seen pointing out to the tourists the direction from which the Confederate army advanced on the first day of battle. Captain Long was a leading battlefield guide for 20 years and the author of a very popular book entitled *The 16th Decisive Battle of the World—Gettysburg*. (Pub. unknown, #2779; c. 1908.)

HARRY W. LONG, SPECIAL TOURIST GUIDE. Here is an early postcard advertising the services of Harry W. Long, battlefield guide. Like his famous father, Capt. James T. Long, he operated from the Eagle Hotel offering his services to tourists. In 1915 the licensed Battlefield Guide Service was established to ensure that visitors would receive reliable and accurate interpretations of the battle and battlefield. (Typographic Union Label; c. 1915.)

SPANGLER'S SPRING. Early visitors to the battlefield would stop at this popular location for a drink from the famous cooling waters of Spangler's Spring. Notice that this photo was taken before the granite structure that now encloses the spring was constructed. (Cunningham & Co.; *c.* 1900.)

SOUVENIR OF DEVIL'S DEN. During the early 1900s, just like today, posing for pictures at Devil's Den was a popular thing to do. Dressed in their finery these individuals had their picture taken as a souvenir remembrance of their visit to the battlefield park. (Real photo card; *c.* 1904.)

POSING AT DEVIL'S DEN. Two couples stand among the large boulders of Devil's Den. Something about this outcropping of massive rocks seems to attract the sightseer. This site has always been a favorite among visitors. (W.H. Tipton, #3531; *c.* 1907.)

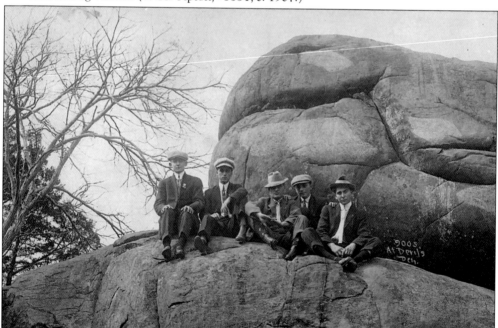

ATOP DEVIL'S DEN. Perched on top of the rocks of Devil's Den, these young men pose for their photograph where Confederate sharpshooters once practiced their deadly art. This real photo postcard is the work of W.H. Tipton of Gettysburg, who was one of the more prolific photographers of the battlefield and published many postcard views of the area. (W.H. Tipton, #9005; *c.* 1907.)

VISITING THE PENNSYLVANIA MONUMENT. Visitors to the battlefield almost always stop to visit this most impressive of memorials. In 1913, just in time for the 50th Anniversary, eight portrait statues of famous individuals were placed in the niches between the Ionic columns that flank the arches. On this early postcard, you can see that these statues have not yet been added. (Union News Co., #1148; c. 1910.)

POSING AT THE PENNSYLVANIA MONUMENT. These four men pose for their picture in front of what is undoubtedly the most photographed monument on the battlefield. This memorial is also the most expensive to have been built at Gettysburg, costing nearly $200,000 at the time of construction. (W.H. Tipton, #7971; *c.* 1910.)

POSING AT THE HIGH WATER MARK. Another site often utilized for souvenir photographs during the early 1900s was the monument to the High Water Mark of the Confederacy. Seen here are three young men striking a pose at this very historic location. They appear to be about the same age as many of those who fought and died here in 1863. (Real photo card, #6106; *c.* 1905.)

DESCRIBING CAMP TO A SWEETHEART, SUNDAY AFTERNOON.

PENN. NATIONAL GUARD CAMP, GETTYSBURG, PA.

NATIONAL GUARD ENCAMPMENT OF 1906. For a number of years the Gettysburg battlefield served as the location for a semiannual encampment of the Pennsylvania National Guard. In July of 1906 this camp site was known as Camp Henderson. Here are seen some of the tenting facilities for the troops, which were comprised of some 10,000 men and officers. (Betts, Brown & Betts; 1906.)

State Militia Encampment—Soldiers Welcoming Young Lady Visitors to Camp.

NATIONAL GUARD ENCAMPMENT OF 1906. During the time of encampment, the National Guard (also known as the State Militia) would drill, train, and be engaged in war games. Towards the end of each encampment, thousands of people would arrive in Gettysburg to see and visit the troops. In this view, some of the soldiers greet two lady visitors. (Pub. unknown; 1906.)

121

NATIONAL GUARD ENCAMPMENT OF 1908. Troopers of the 16th Regiment Company C pose for a group picture during the 1908 encampment of the Pennsylvania National Guard, July 16–25, 1908. These men were part of the 10,000 soldiers involved in training exercises on the site of the former battlefield. (Grove City Postcard Co.; 1908.)

NATIONAL GUARD ENCAMPMENT OF 1908. Company A, 16th Regiment of the Pennsylvania National Guard, are shown here in what was named Camp Alexander M. Hays in July of 1908. Such encampments at Gettysburg were to end when a permanent site was later selected at Mt. Gretna, Pennsylvania. (Grove City Postcard Co.; 1908.)

NATIONAL GUARD ENCAMPMENT OF 1908. Gov. Edwin S. Stuart and Maj. Gen. John A. Wiley, commander of the Pennsylvania National Guard, review the troops from horseback on July 21, 1908. Later that day, a fierce thunderstorm resulted in three soldiers being killed and 40 injured by lightning. (Grove City Postcard Co.; 1908.)

U. S. AMBULANCE CORPS DRILLING, GETTYSBURG, PA.

CAMP COLT. During World War I, a training camp, Camp Colt, was set up within the boundaries of the battlefield park. Here six regiments, like this group from the Ambulance Corps, were trained for combat. In March of 1918 Dwight D. Eisenhower arrived to take command of tank training. Eisenhower was to return years later, after serving as Supreme Commander of Allied Forces in Europe during WW II and President of the United States, to live on a farm next to the battlefield. (Louis Kaufmann & Sons, #A-75882; c. 1917.)

Scene from the Cyclorama Battle Painting, Gettysburg, Pa.

CYCLORAMA. A popular tourist attraction at Gettysburg is the famous Cyclorama. This unique, circular painting of the "Battle of Gettysburg" stands 26 feet high and measures 360 feet in circumference. It was painted in 1884 by French artist Paul Philippoteaux and was brought to Gettysburg in 1913 as part of the 50th Anniversary celebration. (Pub. unknown; *c.* 1915.)

Portion of Cyclorama, "The Battle of Gettysburg,"
Baltimore Street, near National Cemetery, Gettysburg, Pa.

Copyrighted by Albert J. Hahne, Newark, N. J.

CYCLORAMA. The Cyclorama was formally acquired by the National Park Service in 1942 and is still on exhibit today within its own building. This portion of the painting depicts the combat at the Angle where Gen. Lewis Armistead and his soldiers briefly crossed Union lines before the general was killed during Pickett's Charge. (C.T. Photochrom, #R-50006; *c.* 1915.)

JENNIE WADE HOUSE. Pictured here is the Jennie Wade House on Baltimore Street as it appeared in the early 1900s. Over the years, tens of thousands have visited this modest home, which has served as a small museum. Few, however, take the time to visit Jennie's gravesite in nearby Evergreen Cemetery. (Detroit Photographic Co., #7224; 1903.)

VETERANS ON CULP'S HILL. For many years after the battle, evidence of intense artillery and rifle fire could still be seen at numerous sites on the battlefield. Here on Culp's Hill, these bullet-pierced trees stood as "veterans" of the conflict and were reminders to visitors of the bitter engagements that took place on this hillside. (C.A. Blocher, from multiview set; c. 1905.)

23:—Bullet Holes in Fence, Gettysburg, Pa.

BULLET HOLES IN FENCE. Here at the Samuel McCreary house, which faces the Union lines on Cemetery Hill, stands a bullet-riddled fence that serves as evidence of the severity of the fighting. For years such remembrances were preserved for tourists to view when they visited the scenes of former battle. Even today, bullet holes and shell fragments can be seen in the sides of buildings within the town of Gettysburg. (C.A. Blocher, #5877; c. 1920.)

INDEX